I0191416

Understanding & Collaboration Between Religions

Sri Mata Amritanandamayi Devi

Sri Mata Amritanandamayi Devi

Understanding & Collaboration Between Religions

An Address by
Sri Mata Amritanandamayi Devi

Translated By
Swami Amritaswarupananda Puri

Mata Amritanandamayi Mission Trust
Amritapuri P.O., Kollam Dist., Kerala, INDIA 690525

Understanding & Collaboration Between Religions

Sri Mata Amritanandamayi Devi

Published by
  Mata Amritanandamayi Mission Trust
  Amritapuri P.O., Kollam Dist., Kerala, INDIA 690 525
  Email: info@theammashop.org
  Website: www.amritapuri.org
  www.embracingtheworld.org

First editions 2006-2008: 11,000 copies
Sixth edition 2012: 1000 copies

Type setting and layout: Amrita DTP, Amritapuri

Copyright © 2012 by Mata Amritanandamayi Mission Trust

All rights reserved. No part of this publication may be stored in a retrieval system, transmitted, reproduced, transcribed or translated into any language, in any form, by any means without the prior agreement and written permission of the publisher.

Introduction

On May 2nd 2006, Amma delivered the address "Understanding & Collaboration Between Religions" at the Rubin Museum of Art in the Chelsea District of Manhattan as part of the Interfaith Center of New York's Fourth Annual James Parks Morton Interfaith Award Ceremony.

The Interfaith Center of New York (ICNY) bestowed its 2006 award upon Amma for her outstanding work in fostering "inter-religious understanding and respect"—the ICNY's prime directive. "Amma's life is dedicated to acceptance," said the founder of the Rubin Museum, Donald Rubin, when he introduced Amma prior to her receiving the award. "By reaching out and accepting all human beings through the physical act of hugging, she transcends all religions and political divisions. The acceptance and the love that the act of hugging creates is the

◆

healing that we all need. It is the healing that our mothers gave us when we were infants. It is that healing that Amma has given the world."

ICNY was particularly impressed with the massive relief work Amma's Ashram undertook following the 2004 Asian tsunami, and it was interested to hear Amma's thoughts on inter-religious understanding and collaboration in the wake of that experience.

"When natural calamities occur, people's hearts open up, transcending thoughts of caste, religion and politics," Amma said in her address. "Yet, the nonjudgmental attitude and compassion people express during such situations come and go as quickly as a flash of lightening. If, instead, we can manage to keep that flame of compassion ablaze within, it can dispel the darkness surrounding us."

Though Amma delivered her address in her native Malayalam, everyone attending the function was able to listen in English through a simultaneous translation. Amma's words were not the theoretics of a scholar; they were soaked in her enlightenment and personal experience, and, as such, they carried a real weight—one that made a visible impact on everyone assembled.

Although accepting the necessity of religion, Amma continually stressed how important it is for religious practitioners to penetrate to what lies at the core of all faiths. "Just as one sucks the juice from the sugarcane and spits out the stalk, the religious leaders should encourage their followers to imbibe the essence of religion—which is spirituality—and not give over-importance to the external aspects. Unfortunately, today many are eating the stalk and spitting out the essence," Amma said.

Amma also lamented the fact that while saints and sages give importance to spiritual values, their followers often become mired in institutionalism. Amma said, "As a result, the very religions that were meant to spread peace and tranquility by threading people together on the garland of love have become the cause of war and conflict. Due to our ignorance and limited perspective, we are confining the great souls within the tiny cages of religion. In their name, we have locked ourselves inside the prison of the ego, and have proceeded to inflate our egos and fight with one another. If this continues, understanding and collaboration will forever remain a mirage."

In her conclusion, Amma said that a one-word solution for almost all the problems the world is facing today was "compassion" and stressed the importance for all members of all faiths to serve the poor and suffering. "Helping the poor and needy is true prayer," Amma said. "Without compassion, all our efforts will be in vain."

When Amma finished, the hall at the Rubin Museum of Art was filled with applause, and soon the function's attendees were coming forth to individually receive Amma's loving embrace, including many of Amma's fellow honorees.

Swami Amritaswarupananda Puri
Vice Chairman
Mata Amritanandamayi Math

Five others were honored alongside Amma: the 2005 Noble Peace Prize Laureate Dr. Mohammed Elbaradei, Director General of the International Atomic Energy Agency; U.S. Supreme Court Justice Stephen G. Breyer; the renowned American actor Richard Gere, for his work as Director of Healing the Divide and as Chairman of the Board of the International Campaign fo`r Tibet; and the pair of Imam Feisal Abdul Rauf, the Imam of Masjid Al-Farah, and Daisy Khan, the Executive Director of the American Society for Muslim Advancement.

Others whom the ICNY has bestowed its Interfaith Award upon in the past include three Nobel Peace Prize winners—His Holiness the Dalai Lama, Archbishop Desmond Tutu and Shirin Ebadi—as well as former U.S. President Bill Clinton.

(l-r) American Actor Richard Gere, Amma, U.S. Supreme Court Justice Stephen G. Breyer, Daisy Khan, Imam Feisal Abdul Rauf and the Very Reverend James Parks Morton.

"Understanding & Collaboration Between Religions"

Acceptance Speech by
Sri Mata Amritanandamayi Devi
At the Interfaith Center of New York
The Rubin Museum of Art
May 2nd 2006, New York City

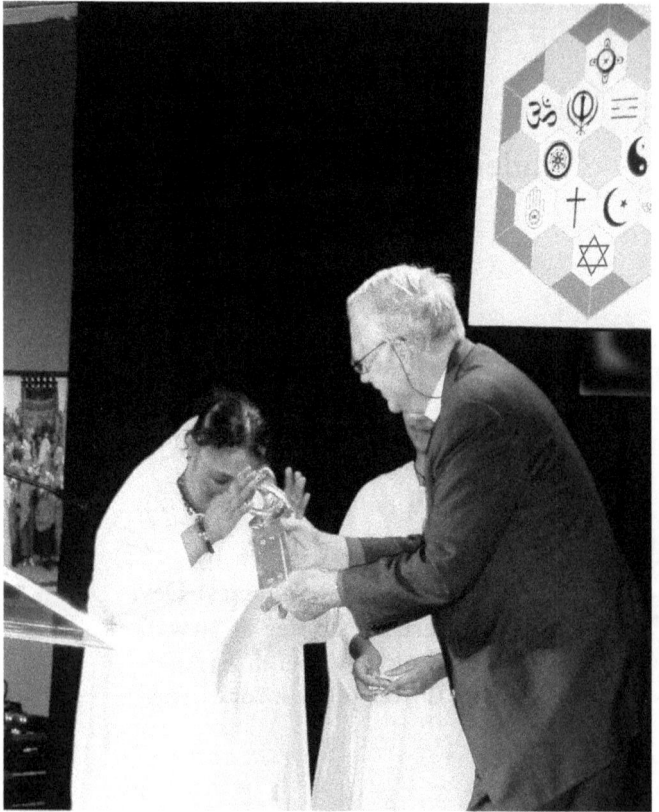

"Understanding & Collaboration Between Religions"

I bow down to everyone here, who are embodiments of Pure Love and Supreme Consciousness.

At the outset, I would like to convey my best wishes to the Interfaith Center of New York. May this organization be able to light the lamp of love and peace in thousands upon thousands of hearts under the able leadership of the Very Reverend James Parks Morton. The Interfaith Center deserves special commendation for its dedicated activities in the wake of the 9/11 tragedy, which claimed the lives of thousands of people, including innocent children. Let me also take this opportunity to express my heartfelt happiness that this conference could be held, and also for the faith that you have vested in me.

In fact, it is only because of the selflessness and self-sacrifice of millions of devotees around

✦

the world that Amma has been able to offer some service to society. Actually, this award and recognition go to them. I am only an instrument.

The topic of today's speech, "Understanding & Collaboration Between Religions," is one that has been discussed at thousands of forums around the world. And while such discussions—and the work of organizations like this one—have brought religions together to some extent, fear and anxiety regarding the world and its future continue to plague our minds.

For this situation to change, we need better understanding and more collaboration between religions. Both religious leaders and heads of state firmly assert this point at meetings such as this. But we are often unable to demonstrate the same firmness in action as we do in word. We share many ideas in these meetings, yet when we try to implement them, we are unable to do so due to the influence of various pressures. A meeting without open hearts is like a parachute that fails to open.

Every religion has two aspects: one is its philosophical teachings as explained in the scriptural texts; the other is spirituality. The former is religion's outer shell, and spirituality, its inner essence. Spirituality is awakening to one's true nature. Those who make the effort to know their True Self are the truly faithful. Whatever one's religion, if one understands the spiritual principles, one can attain the ultimate goal, the realization of one's true nature. If a bottle contains honey, the color of the bottle is irrelevant. On the contrary, if we fail to absorb the spiritual principles, religion will be nothing more than blind faith, shackling us.

The point of religion is to transform our minds. In order for this to happen, one must imbibe spirituality—the inner essence of religion. The unity of hearts is what brings about religious unity. If our hearts fail to unite, instead of coming together as a team, we will drift apart, and our efforts will be fragmented.

Religion points the way, like a road sign. The goal is spiritual experience.

For example, pointing to a tree, a person says, "Look at that tree. Do you see the fruit hanging on that branch? If you eat it, you will

❖

attain immortality!" Then, what we should do is climb the tree, pick the fruit and eat it. If, instead, we hold on to the person's finger, we will never be able to enjoy the fruit. This is akin to clinging to the words of the scriptures, rather than grasping the spiritual principles to which they point.

Just as one sucks the juice from the sugar-cane and spits out the stalk, the religious leaders should encourage their followers to imbibe the essence of religion—which is spirituality—and not give over-importance to the external aspects. Unfortunately, today many are eating the stalk and spitting out the essence.

The power of religion lies in spirituality. Spirituality is the cement that fortifies the edifice of society. Practicing religion and living life without assimilating spirituality is like constructing a tower by simply piling up bricks without ever using any cement. It will easily crumble. Religious faith without spirituality becomes lifeless, like a part of the body cut off from the flow of circulation.

Atomic energy can be used either to create

or to destroy. We can use it to generate electricity for the benefit of the world. We can also produce an atomic bomb that destroys everything. The choice is ours. Imbibing the spiritual aspect of religion is like generating electricity from the atom, whereas religion devoid of a spiritual perspective will lead to grave danger.

Even in olden times, the caste system and other socio-religious divisions existed in various cultures. Back then, such divisions were out in the open, for one and all to see. Today, on the other hand, we speak as if we are extremely aware of the importance of religious unity and equality, but within us hatred and the desire for revenge continue to rage. In olden times, the problems were predominantly on the gross level, but now they are on the subtle level, and for that very reason they are more powerful and pervasive.

Amma is reminded of a story. There was a notorious criminal in a city. Every day at 7 p.m. he would come and loiter at a particular street corner, where he would accost and insult the women and young girls who passed by. Out of fear, no woman would pass that way after sunset; they would hide behind the closed doors of their houses. Several years passed like this, and then, one day, the criminal suddenly died.

However, even after the criminal died, the women of that area continued to remain indoors after sunset. Perplexed, some people asked why no one was venturing outside. The women responded, "When he was alive, we could see him with our own eyes. We knew when and where he was standing. But now it's his ghost that is assaulting us. So, now, he can attack us anywhere, at any time! Being subtle, he is more powerful and pervasive." Similar is the case with today's socio-religious divisions.

In fact, religion is a constraint created by humans. At birth, we had no conditioning or limitations regarding religion or language. These have been taught to us, conditioning us over time. Just as a small plant needs a fence, this conditioning is necessary to a certain extent. Once the seedling grows into a tree, it transcends the fence. Similarly, we must be able to go beyond our religious conditioning and become "unconditional."

There are three things that make a human humane: 1. the intense desire to know the meaning and depth of life through discriminative thinking; 2. the miraculous ability to give love; 3. the power to be joyful and to give joy to others. Religion should help people realize all three of these. Only then will religion and humans become complete.

Whereas great souls give importance to spiritual values, their followers often give more importance to institutions and organizations. As a result, the very religions that were meant to spread peace and tranquility by threading people together on the garland of love have become the cause of war and conflict.

Due to our ignorance and limited perspective, we are confining the great souls within the tiny cages of religion. In their name, we have locked ourselves inside the prison of the ego, and have proceeded to inflate our egos and fight with one another. If this continues, understanding and collaboration will forever remain a mirage.

Once, two men on a bicycle-built-for-two were trying to ascend a steep hill. Though they struggled with all their might, they traveled only a short distance. Tired and weary, at one point they got off the bicycle to rest. Out of breath and covered in sweat, the man riding in front said, "What a hill! No matter how hard we pedal, we're not getting anywhere. I'm beat, and my back is killing me!"

Hearing this, the man riding in back said, "Hey, buddy, you think you're tired! If I hadn't kept the brake on the whole time, we would have slid all the way back down!"

Consciously or unconsciously, this is what we are doing today in the name of mutual understanding and collaboration. We don't open our hearts due to the deep-rooted distrust we have for each other.

In reality, the principles of love, compassion and unity are at the heart of all religious teachings.

Christianity says, "Love thy neighbor as

thyself." Hinduism says, "We should pray that others may have what we want for ourselves." Islam says, "If your enemy's donkey falls ill, you must take care of it." Judaism says, "Hating one's neighbor is equal to hating one's self." Though expressed in different ways, the principle conveyed here is the same. The import of all these sayings is that: As the same Soul, or Atman, abides in all things, we must see and serve all as One. It is people's distorted intellect that makes them interpret these principles in a limited way.

Amma remembers a story. Once, a renowned artist painted a picture of an enchanting young woman. Whoever saw the painting fell in love with her. Some of them asked the painter if the woman was his beloved. When he said no, each one of them adamantly insisted on marrying her and wouldn't allow anyone else to do so.

They demanded, "We want to know where to find this beautiful lady."

The painter told them, "I'm sorry, but actually, I've never seen her. She has no nationality, religion or language. What you see in her is not the beauty of an individual, either. I simply gave

◆

eyes, a nose and a form to the beauty I beheld within me."

But none of them believed the painter's words. They angrily accused him, saying, "You are lying to us. You just want to make her your own!"

The painter calmly told them, "No, please don't take this painting at surface level. Even if you search all over the world, you won't find her—yet she is the quintessence of all beauty."

Nonetheless, ignoring the words of the painter, the people became infatuated with the paint and the painting. In their intense desire to possess the young woman, they quarreled and fought with each other and finally perished.

We, too, are like this. Today, we are searching for a God who dwells only in pictures and scriptures. In that search, we have lost our way.

The scriptures say that each of us sees the world through tinted glasses. We see in the world that which we project. If we look with eyes of hatred and vengeance, the world will appear exactly that way to us. But if we look with eyes of love and compassion, we will see nothing but God's beauty everywhere.

Amma has heard of an experiment conducted to ascertain whether or not this world really is as we perceive it. The researchers gave a young man a pair of glasses that distorted his vision. They then instructed him to wear the glasses continuously for seven days. For the first three days, he was very restless, as his perception of everything was quite disturbing. But after that, his eyes became fully adjusted to the glasses, and the pain and discomfort completely disappeared. What had at first made the world seem strange and distorted, later seemed normal to him.

In the same way, each of us is wearing a different type of glasses. It is through these glasses that we view the world and religion. We react accordingly. Because of this, we are often unable to even see people as human beings.

Amma remembers an experience a religious leader shared with her many years ago. He went to attend a function at a hospital in Hyderabad, India. As he got out of the car and was walking towards the hospital, he saw that many women

◆

were lined up on both sides of his path to receive him in the traditional style—holding oil lamps and raw rice. As he walked into their midst, they soaked the rice in the oil and flung it in his face. He told Amma, "Far from being a warm welcome, it was rather one of anger and opposition. I gestured to them to stop, covering my face with my hands, but they continued anyway."

Later, he inquired whether the people lined up to receive him believed in God. The owner of the hospital told him that they were believers and were his staff. He replied, "I don't think so, because I could feel anger and vindictiveness in their behavior."

Suspecting something, the owner sent someone to investigate the incident. This is what he saw: the people who had welcomed the religious leader were assembled in a room, laughing. With contempt in her voice, one of them loudly boasted, "I really gave it to that devil!"

Actually, the staff belonged to a different religion. Since their boss had told them to do so, they had no choice but to receive the guest. But they did not have any understanding of true religion or spiritual culture. In fact, their mind-set was one wherein people of different faiths were actually not humans, but devils.

There are two types of ego. One is the ego of power and money. But the second type is more destructive. That is the ego that feels, "My religion and viewpoint alone are correct. All others are wrong and unnecessary. I won't tolerate anything else." This is like saying, "My mother is good; yours is a prostitute!" This kind of thinking and conduct are the cause of all religious friction. Unless we eradicate these two types of ego, it will be difficult to bring about peace in the world.

The willingness to listen to others, the ability to understand them and the broad-mindedness to accept even those who disagree with us—these are the signs of true spiritual culture. Unfortunately, these qualities are exactly what are missing from the world today.

Nevertheless, when natural calamities occur, people's hearts open up, transcending thoughts of caste, religion and politics. When the tsunami struck South Asia, all barriers of religion and nationality disappeared. All hearts ached in compassion for the victims. All eyes shed tears along with them. And all hands reached out to dry those tears and to help the people.

Countless are the occasions when my heart and soul have been filled, seeing atheists and people belonging to different political parties and religions working day and night alongside residents of our ashram [monastery] in a spirit of self-sacrifice. Yet, the nonjudgmental attitude and compassion people express during such situations come and go as quickly as a flash of lightening. If, instead, we can manage to keep that flame of compassion ablaze within, it can dispel the darkness surrounding us. In this way, may the trickle of compassion within us grow into a torrential flow. Let us transform that spark of love into an effulgence, blazing like the sun. This will create a heaven on earth. The capacity to do this dwells within all of us; it is our birthright and true nature.

Regardless of its color, if we fill a balloon with helium, it will soar up to the sky. Similarly, people of all religions can soar to great heights if they fill their hearts with love.

Amma remembers a story. Once, the colors of the world gathered together. Each one claimed, "I am the most important and beloved color." The conversation culminated in a quarrel.

Green proudly declared, "Indeed, I am the most important color. I am the sign of life. Trees, vines—all of nature is my color. Need I say more?"

Blue interrupted, "Hey, stop your blabbering! You are only talking about the Earth. Don't you see the sky and the ocean? They are all blue in color. And water is the substratum of life. Hail to me, the color of infinity and love."

Hearing this, Red shouted, "Enough is enough! Everybody shut up! I am the ruler of you all—I am blood. I am the color of valor and courage. Without me, there is no life."

Amidst this shouting, White softly said, "You have all stated your cases. Now, I have just one thing to say: don't forget the truth—that I am the substratum of all colors."

❖

Nevertheless, many more colors came forward, all extolling their greatness and supremacy over the others. Gradually, what began as a mere exchange of words developed into a verbal battle. The colors were even poised to destroy each other.

Suddenly, the sky became dark. There was thunder and lightning, followed by a heavy downpour. The water level rose rapidly. Trees were uprooted, and all of nature was in turmoil.

Trembling with fear, the colors helplessly cried out, "Save us!" Just then they heard a voice from the heavens, "You colors! Where are your ego and false pride now? You who were foolishly fighting for supremacy, are now trembling with fear, unable to protect even your own lives. All you claim as yours can perish in an instant. You must understand one thing—though different, each of you is beyond compare. God has created each one of you with a different purpose. To save yourselves, you must stand hand-in-hand in unity. If you stand together in oneness, you can soar up and stretch across the sky. You can become the rainbow with all seven colors, harmoniously standing side-by-side—the symbol of peace and beauty, the sign of hope for tomorrow. From that height, all differences disappear and you see everything as one. May your unity and harmony become an inspiration for all."

Whenever we behold an exquisite rainbow, may we feel inspired to work together as a team, with mutual understanding and appreciation.

Religions are the flowers arranged for worshipping God. How beautiful it would be if they stood together! They would then spread the fragrance of peace throughout the whole world.

Religious leaders should come forward to sing the peace song of universal unity and love. They should become like mirrors for the world. The mirror is cleaned not for its own sake, but so that those who look in it are able to better clean their own face. Religious emissaries must become role models. The example that religious leaders set will determine the purity of their followers' actions and thoughts. Only when noble-minded people practice religious ideals will their followers imbibe the same spirit and feel inspired to act nobly.

In a way, everyone should become a role model, because someone or the other will always be taking us as an example. It is our duty to consider those who look up to us. In a world of role models, there will neither be war nor weapons. They will be reduced to nothing more than a bad dream we had long, long ago. Arms and ammunitions will be rendered artifacts to be kept in some museum—symbols of our past, when humans erred from the path leading to their goal.

Our mistake is that we have become deluded by the superficial aspects of religion. Let us rectify this error. Together, let us realize the heart of religion—universal love, purity of heart, beholding oneness everywhere. We live in an age when the entire world is reducing into a global village. What we need is not mere religious tolerance, but deep mutual understanding. We should do away with misunderstanding and mistrust. Let us bid farewell to the dark age of rivalry and mark the beginning of a new era of creative, inter-religious cooperation. We have just stepped into the third millennium. May

the future generation call this the millennium of religious friendship and cooperation.

Amma would like to propose a few suggestions for everyone's consideration:

1) A one-word solution for almost all the problems the world is facing today is "compassion." The essence of all religions is in being compassionate to others. Religious leaders should highlight the importance of compassion through the example of their own lives. Nothing is more scarce in the world today than role models. Religious leaders should come forward to fill this vacuum.

2) Due to our exploitation of nature and general lack of awareness, pollution is destroying the earth. Religious leaders should conduct campaigns to create awareness regarding the importance of environmental protection.

3) We might not be able to avert natural calamities. And as human beings have no control over their ego, it might not be possible to totally prevent war and other conflicts either. But

◆

if we make a firm resolve, surely we can eradicate hunger and poverty. All religious leaders should try their best to achieve this goal.

4) To foster inter-religious understanding, every religion should start centers wherein the teachings of other faiths are studied in depth. This should be done with an expansive vision, not with any ulterior motives.

5) Just as the sun doesn't need the light of a candle, God doesn't need anything from us. Helping the poor and needy is true prayer. Without compassion, all our efforts will be in vain—like pouring milk into a dirty vessel. All religions should emphasize the importance of compassionately serving the poor and suffering.

Let us pray and work together to create a joyous tomorrow, free from conflict, where religions work together in happiness, peace and love.

Sri Mata Amritanandamayi Devi

❖

May the tree of our life be firmly rooted
in the soil of love.
Let good deeds be the leaves on that tree;
May words of kindness form its flowers;
May peace be its fruit.
Let us grow and unfold as one family,
united in love—
so that we may rejoice and
celebrate our oneness,
in a world where peace and
contentment prevail.

ॐ

Book Catalog
By Author

Sri Mata Amritanandamayi Devi
108 Quotes On Faith
108 Quotes On Love
Compassion, The Only Way To Peace:
    Paris Speech
Cultivating Strength And Vitality
Living In Harmony
May Peace And Happiness Prevail:
    Barcelona Speech
May Your Hearts Blossom:
    Chicago Speech
Practice Spiritual Values And Save The
    World: Delhi Speech
The Awakening Of Universal
    Motherhood: Geneva Speech
The Eternal Truth
The Infinite Potential Of Women:
    Jaipur Speech
Understanding And Collaboration
    Between Religions
Unity Is Peace: Interfaith Speech

Swami Amritaswarupananda Puri
Ammachi: A Biography
Awaken Children, Volumes 1-9
From Amma's Heart
Mother Of Sweet Bliss
The Color Of Rainbow

Swami Jnanamritananda Puri
Eternal Wisdom, Volumes 1-2

Swami Paramatmananda Puri
On The Road To Freedom Volumes 1-2
Talks, Volumes 1-6

Swami Purnamritananda Puri
Unforgettable Memories

Swami Ramakrishnananda Puri
Eye Of Wisdom
Racing Along The Razor's Edge
Secret Of Inner Peace
The Blessed Life
The Timeless Path
Ultimate Success

Swamini Krishnamrita Prana
Love Is The Answer
Sacred Journey
The Fragrance Of Pure Love
Torrential Love

M.A. Center Publications
1,000 Names Commentary
Archana Book (Large)
Archana Book (Small)
Being With Amma
Bhagavad Gita
Bhajanamritam, Volumes 1-6
Embracing The World
For My Children
Immortal Light
Lead Us To Purity
Lead Us To The Light
Man And Nature
My First Darshan
Puja: The Process Of Ritualistic
    Worship
Sri Lalitha Trishati Stotram

Amma's Websites

AMRITAPURI—Amma's Home Page
Teachings, Activities, Ashram Life, eServices, Yatra, Blogs and News
http://www.amritapuri.org

AMMA (Mata Amritanandamayi)
About Amma, Meeting Amma, Global Charities, Groups and Activities and Teachings
http://www.amma.org

EMBRACING THE WORLD®
Basic Needs, Emergencies, Environment, Research and News
http://www.embracingtheworld.org

AMRITA UNIVERSITY
About, Admissions, Campuses, Academics, Research, Global and News
http://www.amrita.edu

THE AMMA SHOP—Embracing the World® Books & Gifts Shop
Blog, Books, Complete Body, Home & Gifts, Jewelry, Music and Worship
http://www.theammashop.org

IAM—Integrated Amrita Meditation Technique®
Meditation Taught Free of Charge to the Public, Students, Prisoners and Military
http://www.amma.org/groups/north-america/projects/iam-meditation-classes

AMRITA PUJA
Types and Benefits of Pujas, Brahmasthanam Temple, Astrology Readings, Ordering Pujas
http://www.amritapuja.org

GREENFRIENDS
Growing Plants, Building Sustainable Environments, Education and Community Building
http://www.amma.org/groups/north-america/projects/green-friends

FACEBOOK
This is the Official Facebook Page to Connect with Amma
https://www.facebook.com/MataAmritanandamayi

DONATION PAGE
Please Help Support Amma's Charities Here:
http://www.amma.org/donations

www.ingramcontent.com/pod-product-compliance
Lightning Source LLC
Chambersburg PA
CBHW051000030426
42339CB00007B/419